Micha...

RY. Crew Skills

Illustrations by Steve Lucas

www.rya.org.uk

© RYA
This edition published 2014
Reprinted February 2015, March 2016,
March 2017, April 2018
First published as
RYA Competent Crew
The Royal Yachting Association
RYA House, Ensign Way,
Hamble, Southampton,
Hampshire SO31 4YA
Tel: 02380 604100
Web: www.rya.org.uk
Follow us on Twitter @RYAPublications
or on YouTube

We welcome feedback on our
publications at publications@rya.org.uk

You can check content updates for RYA
publications at
www.rya.org.uk/go/bookschangelog

ISBN 978-1-906435905
RYA Order Code: CCPCN

Cover design: Pete Galvin
Acknowledgements: Jon Mendez
Typeset: Creativebyte
Proofreading and indexing: Alan Thatcher
Printed in China through World Print Ltd

Sustainable
Forests

Foreword

If you have picked up this book there is a good chance that you have been 'bitten by the sailing bug'! If that hasn't yet happened, it is only a matter of time. Whether your aspiration is to drift quietly around your local harbour or to skipper a round the world race yacht the wonderful world of boating has something to offer everyone.

This book is intended to support the five-day RYA Competent Crew course. It is designed to assist you in understanding new concepts and in particular to help you remember some of the unique terminology that is used in the world of boating. It is an excellent starting point for those undertaking their first boating experience or those returning to the sport after a long time away from it.

Learning the basic crewing skills in the RYA Competent Crew course is the ideal way to build confidence in your own abilities in a safe and supportive environment before moving on to more challenging experiences.

As your experience develops there are more advanced courses to try and over 100 other RYA publications to assist you in further developing your knowledge.

Happy boating and enjoy your course!

Richard Falk
RYA Director of Training

Contents

Introduction

Over 12,000 people, most with absolutely no sailing experience, successfully complete an RYA Competent Crew course every year. It gives a great insight into the world of sailing in larger boats and the enjoyment that it brings.

The courses are run by over 300 RYA Recognised Training Centres around the UK and overseas. Using an RYA Recognised Training Centre will ensure that you are taught to the RYA's high standards, and your course will be safe, informative and enjoyable.

This book has been written using the cumulative experience of hundreds of experienced sailing instructors. The techniques shown/described are tried and tested and are suitable for most types of cruising boat. We hope that you enjoy the book and find it useful. Good sailing!

Nautical Terms

It's worth learning the nautical terms because they are exact definitions of technical features. This means no confusion, and they will help you understand the sport and learn more quickly. The nautical terms are used throughout this book. Try to use them afloat – they are unambiguous and really help all to understand.

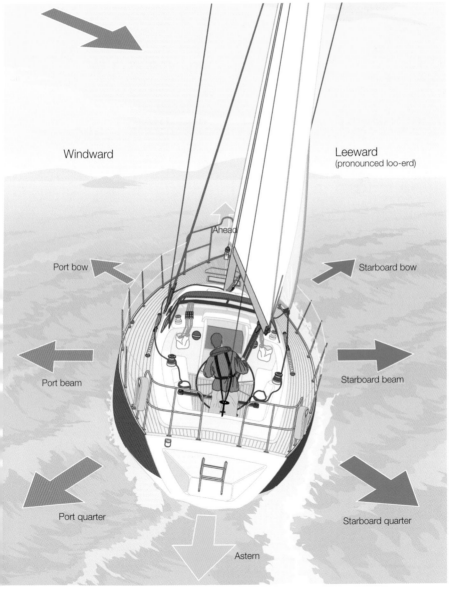

Windward

Leeward
(pronounced loo-erd)

Ahead

Port bow

Starboard bow

Port beam

Starboard beam

Port quarter

Starboard quarter

Astern

Different Types of Yacht

Sailing boats come in all shapes and sizes and can be highly specialised. Nearly all boats are some form of compromise and designers are always attempting to strike the right balance between comfort and performance.

CRUISER RACER
These boats mix good performance with comfort. When racing, heavy items can be removed from the boat. Many owners will have two sets of sails – one for cruising and one for racing.

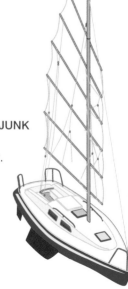

MOTOR SAILER
The boats are a compromise between sailing performance and comfort, with a powerful engine to get you there in adverse winds.

TRADITIONAL CRAFT
Many people enjoy sailing on this type of vessel. Used in the past for coastal trade.

SMALL CRUISER WITH JUNK RIG AND BILGE KEELS
Rig style from the Far East. Simple to sail and easily controlled by one person.

SMALL RACING YACHT OR KEELBOAT

Designed for day racing, mostly inshore. These boats are light, high performance, demanding and exciting to sail.

MEDIUM OR LARGE CRUISING YACHT

Usually comfortable, easy to handle, reliable and safe but still with a reasonable sailing performance.

CRUISING CATAMARAN

Multihulls can provide a combination of good performance and comfort. Many have undertaken long ocean passages. Great downwind.

CRUISING YACHT WITH WINDSURFER RIG

This type of rig is easy to handle when short-handed.

RACING TRIMARAN (3 HULLS) OR CATAMARAN (2 HULLS)

This is about as fast as you'll get to go on a sailing boat. Fast, exciting, unforgiving – for experienced sailors only!

SQUARE RIGGER

Restored or newly built boats are used for sail training and 'Tall Ships' events.

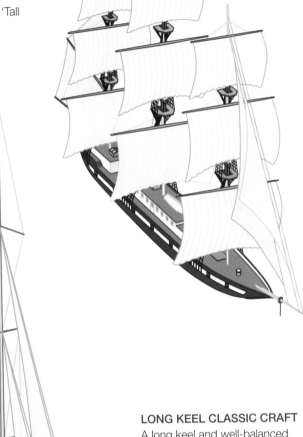

LONG KEEL CLASSIC CRAFT

A long keel and well-balanced sails make these boats hold a very straight and steady course at sea – but under power in a marina they can be hard to manoeuvre.

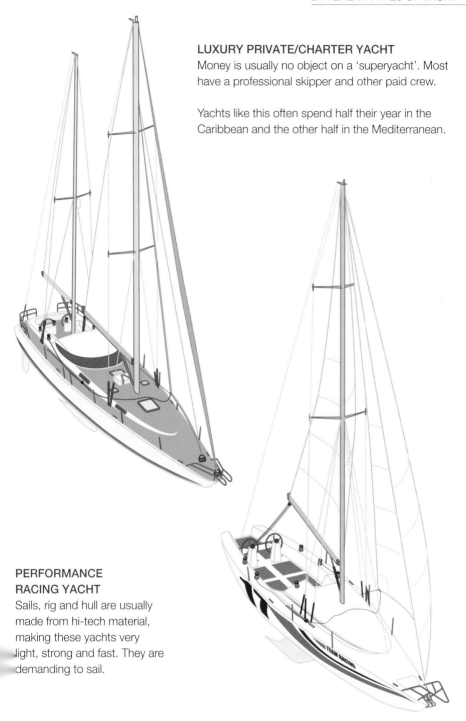

LUXURY PRIVATE/CHARTER YACHT

Money is usually no object on a 'superyacht'. Most have a professional skipper and other paid crew.

Yachts like this often spend half their year in the Caribbean and the other half in the Mediterranean.

PERFORMANCE RACING YACHT

Sails, rig and hull are usually made from hi-tech material, making these yachts very light, strong and fast. They are demanding to sail.

Different Types of Power Vessel

FLYBRIDGE MOTOR CRUISER
Widely used in leisure cruising
and can also be commonly
chartered.

SEMI-DISPLACEMENT VESSEL
Commonly used as pilot boats
and by harbourmasters, but also
seen within the leisure market.

RIB (RIGID INFLATABLE BOAT)

Light, fast and seaworthy, these
are used commercially and
for pleasure.

DISPLACEMENT VESSEL

Traditionally load-carrying and
working vessels, these are
sometimes used for
training.

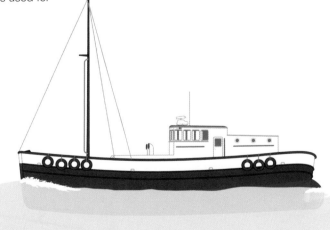

Parts of a Sailing Boat

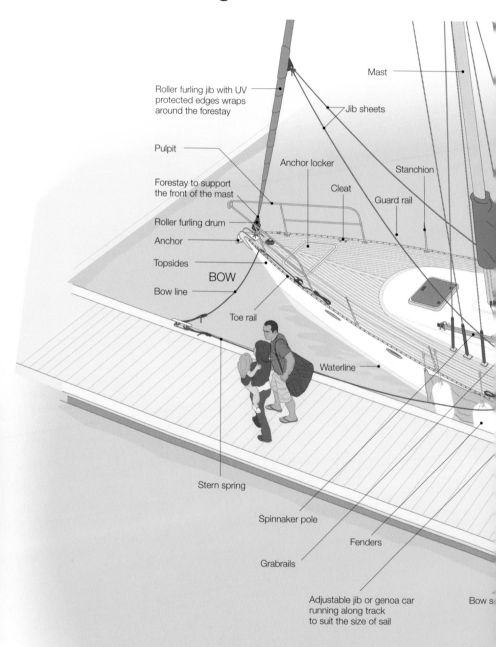

Roller furling jib with UV protected edges wraps around the forestay

Pulpit

Forestay to support the front of the mast

Roller furling drum

Anchor

Topsides

Bow line

BOW

Toe rail

Anchor locker

Cleat

Mast

Jib sheets

Stanchion

Guard rail

Waterline

Stern spring

Spinnaker pole

Grabrails

Fenders

Adjustable jib or genoa car running along track to suit the size of sail

Bow s

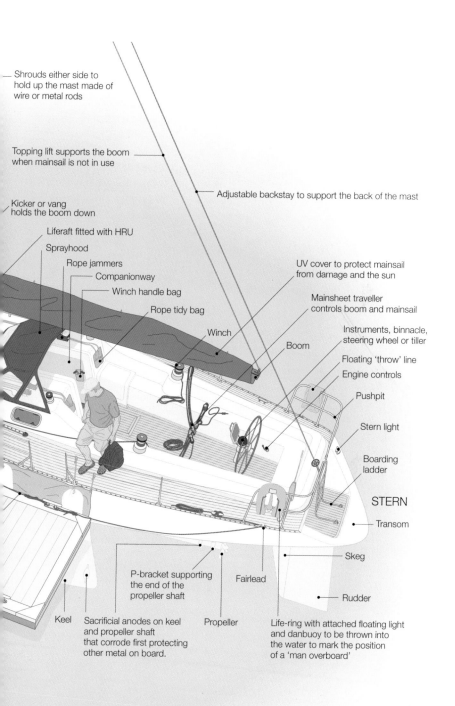

Shrouds either side to hold up the mast made of wire or metal rods

Topping lift supports the boom when mainsail is not in use

Adjustable backstay to support the back of the mast

Kicker or vang holds the boom down

Liferaft fitted with HRU

Sprayhood

Rope jammers

Companionway

Winch handle bag

Rope tidy bag

UV cover to protect mainsail from damage and the sun

Mainsheet traveller controls boom and mainsail

Winch

Boom

Instruments, binnacle, steering wheel or tiller

Floating 'throw' line

Engine controls

Pushpit

Stern light

Boarding ladder

STERN

Transom

Skep

P-bracket supporting the end of the propeller shaft

Fairlead

Rudder

Keel

Sacrificial anodes on keel and propeller shaft that corrode first protecting other metal on board.

Propeller

Life-ring with attached floating light and danbuoy to be thrown into the water to mark the position of a 'man overboard'

MASTHEAD

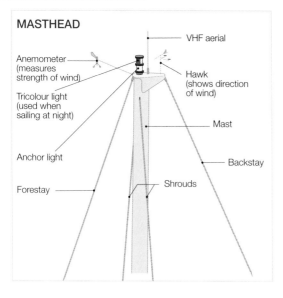

VHF aerial

Anemometer
(measures
strength of wind)

Hawk
(shows direction
of wind)

Tricolour light
(used when
sailing at night)

Mast

Anchor light

Backstay

Forestay

Shrouds

TYPES OF JIB

On a sailing boat you will need to learn the parts of the sails and rigging – it will really help you understand sailing.

Roller-furling

One sail is used for all wind strengths. It can be made smaller when the wind increases by pulling on the furling line from the cockpit. This wraps the sail around the forestay.

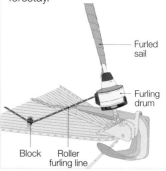

Furled sail

Furling drum

Block   Roller furling line

Luff groove sail

Different-size jibs can be fed into grooves in a head foil. This gives a sail shape that is more aerodynamically efficient for a better sailing performance.

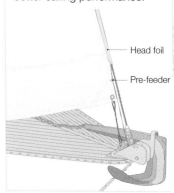

Head foil

Pre-feeder

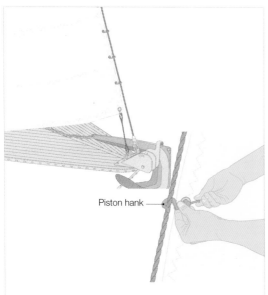

Piston hank

Hanked-on jib

Different-size jibs are attached to the forestay by piston hanks. The sail is securely attached on the boat and is less likely to be lost over the side when hoisting or dropping the sail.

RIGGING AND SAILS

Adjustable backstay

Tensioning the backstay bends the mast back. This flattens the shape of the mainsail and helps to de-power it in strong winds.

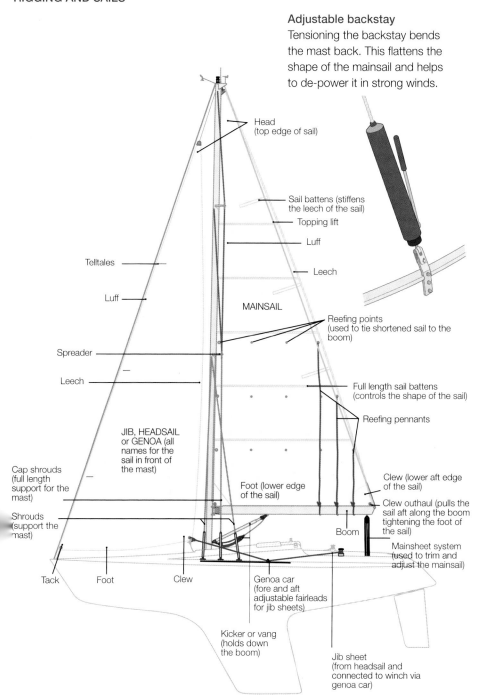

Head
(top edge of sail)

Sail battens (stiffens the leech of the sail)

Topping lift

Luff

Telltales

Leech

Luff

MAINSAIL

Reefing points
(used to tie shortened sail to the boom)

Spreader

Leech

Full length sail battens
(controls the shape of the sail)

Reefing pennants

JIB, HEADSAIL
or GENOA (all names for the sail in front of the mast)

Cap shrouds
(full length support for the mast)

Foot (lower edge of the sail)

Clew (lower aft edge of the sail)

Clew outhaul (pulls the sail aft along the boom tightening the foot of the sail)

Shrouds
(support the mast)

Boom

Mainsheet system
(used to trim and adjust the mainsail)

Tack

Foot

Clew

Genoa car
(fore and aft adjustable fairleads for jib sheets)

Kicker or vang
(holds down the boom)

Jib sheet
(from headsail and connected to winch via genoa car)

How a reefing pennant is rigged

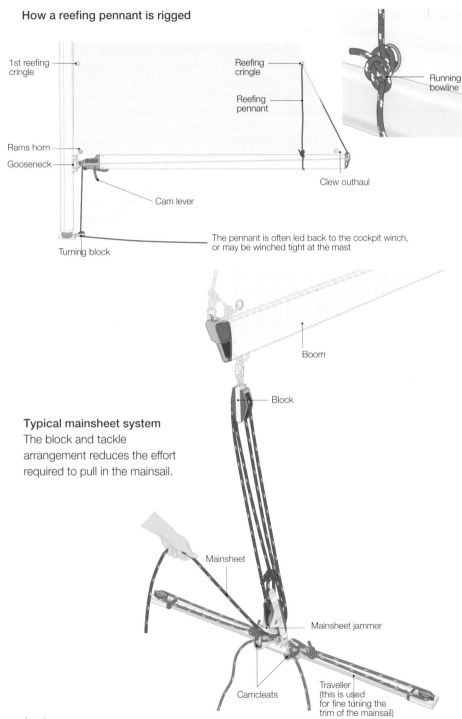

1st reefing cringle

Reefing cringle

Reefing pennant

Running bowline

Rams horn

Gooseneck

Clew outhaul

Cam lever

Turning block

The pennant is often led back to the cockpit winch, or may be winched tight at the mast

Boom

Block

Typical mainsheet system
The block and tackle arrangement reduces the effort required to pull in the mainsail.

Mainsheet

Mainsheet jammer

Camcleats

Traveller (this is used for fine tuning the trim of the mainsail)

Kicker or vang

When under sail, the kicker helps to stop the boom and the mainsail from lifting up too much when the wind is from astern.

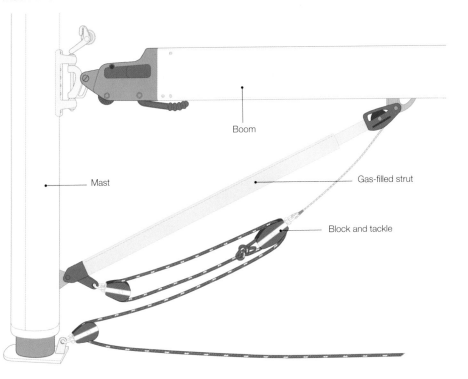

Boom

Mast

Gas-filled strut

Block and tackle

Parts of a Motor Boat

A typical motor cruiser.

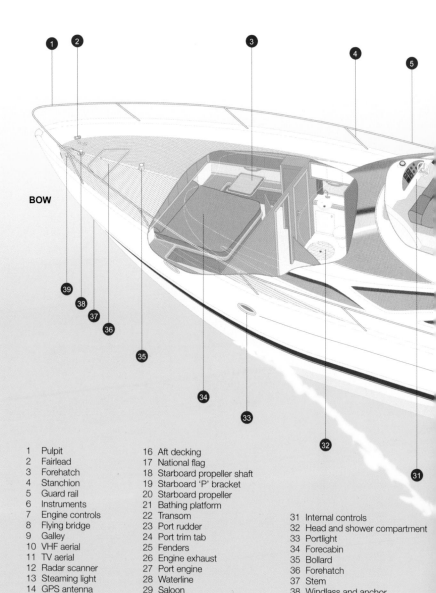

BOW

1 Pulpit	16 Aft decking	
2 Fairlead	17 National flag	
3 Forehatch	18 Starboard propeller shaft	
4 Stanchion	19 Starboard 'P' bracket	
5 Guard rail	20 Starboard propeller	
6 Instruments	21 Bathing platform	
7 Engine controls	22 Transom	
8 Flying bridge	23 Port rudder	
9 Galley	24 Port trim tab	
10 VHF aerial	25 Fenders	31 Internal controls
11 TV aerial	26 Engine exhaust	32 Head and shower compartment
12 Radar scanner	27 Port engine	33 Portlight
13 Steaming light	28 Waterline	34 Forecabin
14 GPS antenna	29 Saloon	35 Bollard
15 Liferaft	30 Port navigation light	36 Forehatch
		37 Stem
		38 Windlass and anchor
		39 Cleat

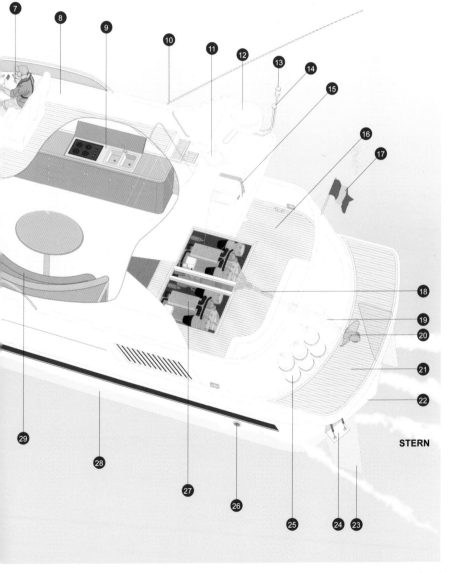

STERN

WINCHES

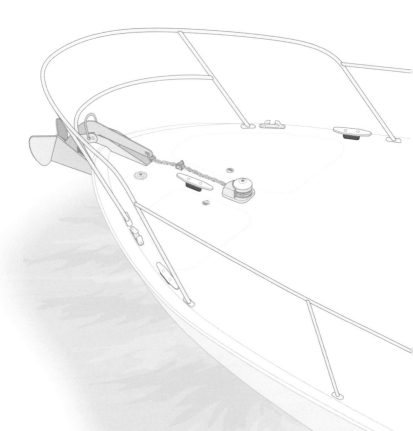

Winches are typically located on the bow by the anchor locker for easy deployment. They are operated from the wheelhouse or on deck, using a hand-held or foot control.

MASTHEAD

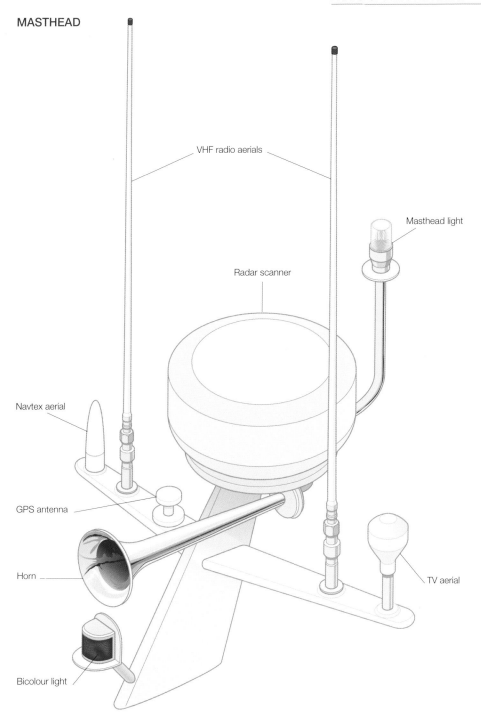

VHF radio aerials

Masthead light

Radar scanner

Navtex aerial

GPS antenna

Horn

TV aerial

Bicolour light

Knots

Just a few knots will get you sailing. They are easy to tie with a bit of practice and you will find them very useful.

Figure-of-eight
Used as a stopper knot to prevent a rope running through a car or jammer.

Clove hitch
For tying on fenders or other uses such as lashing the tiller amidships.

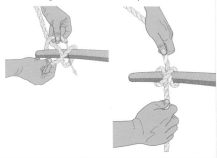

Rolling hitch
Used for temporarily relieving the strain on a working rope, e.g. if you have a riding turn (jam) on a winch.

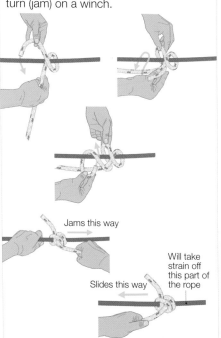

Jams this way

Slides this way

Will take strain off this part of the rope

Bowline
Makes a loop in the end of a rope. Used to attach the jib sheets or to make a loop for mooring.

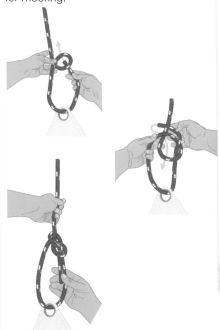

Round turn and two half-hitches
A versatile knot with many uses, such as securing a mooring line to a ring or hanging a fender.

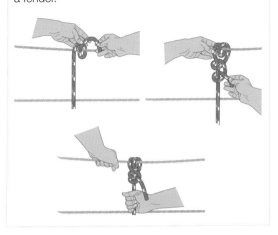

Single sheet bend
Used to join two ropes – useful to lengthen a mooring line.

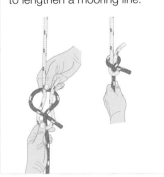

Double sheet bend
More secure and is also used to tie a smaller line to a larger one.

Reef knot
Useful to tie in reefs to tidy the sail – but not secure enough for mooring lines.

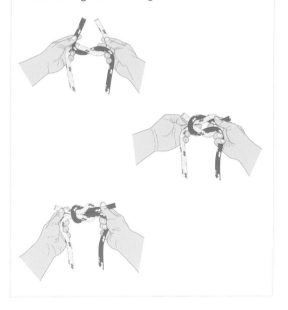

Ropework

Making fast to a cleat

Take the rope round the cleat, add one or more figure-of-eights and make another round turn to secure. 'O-X-O' is a good way to remember this.

Bowlines dipped through and onto the bollard – easy for any vessel to leave.

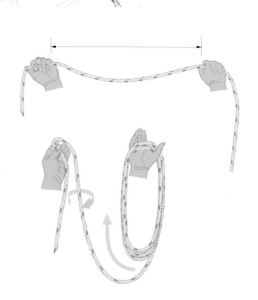

Bowline on a ring – the round turn reduces the chafe.

Coiling a rope

1. Pulling your arms apart the same amount for each coil will help you make even loops.

2. Coil the rope clockwise into your right hand and twist your left wrist away from you before you place each loop in your right hand.

3. When reaching the end, wrap some rope tightly round the coil, near the top.

4. Push a loop through the top.

5. Bring the loop over the top.

6. Pull tight. This is a good secure method of stowing ropes that will not be hung up.

7. Hang the rope up with a clove hitch.

To secure a halyard to a cleat
Coil the halyard starting at the cleat and work towards the loose end of the rope.

1. Put a hand through the coil. Grab the rope coming from the cleat. Pull a loop through the coil.

2. Turn the loop over.

3. Push the loop over the cleat and pull the coil downwards.

Before throwing a rope
Split the coil into two with slack between. Throw the first half and release the second immediately after. This will reach the greatest distance and make the rope easier to catch.

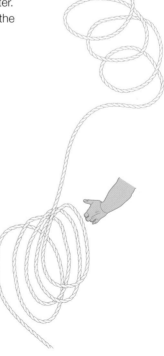

Preparing the Sails for the Sea

Getting the sails up can be hard work. However, with teamwork and practice at sweating and winching it becomes second nature.

Sweating up a halyard

1. Pull out with the right hand while keeping the rope secure on the cleat with the left hand. Do not wrap the rope round your hand.

2. Take up the slack with the left hand down as you pull down with the right.

Using a block with a cam cleat
Pull the rope up to jam it – pull through the jammer to tighten.

Pull the rope down to release it from the jammer. You can then ease the rope out. Keep your fingers well away from the jammer.

Using rope jammers
A rope can be tightened by pulling or winching through a closed jamming cleat.

Do not release under load – keep fingers away.

To release a rope in a jammer
Winch in the rope a little first, then hold the tension on the winch and fully open the jammer.

Using winches

1. Load a rope round the winch clockwise.

Use a flat hand to ease the rope out.

A self-tailing winch holds the rope in a groove at the top.

2. Keep the tension on and put two turns round the winch. Have your little finger nearest the winch and keep sliding the hand away from the winch.

For a fast release, spin the rope vertically upwards to clear the turns off the winch and then let go! Make sure the sheet will run out smoothly.

3. Keep the tension on while using the winch handle. Many winches have two gears.

Never wrap rope round your hand when holding it, pulling on it, or using a winch. Keep hands and fingers away from winches and jammers.

Crew work together to provide tension on the sheet. Watch the sail and wind the winch.

Main

1. Take off the mainsail cover. Fold and stow it.

2. Attach the main halyard making sure it is led correctly from the masthead to the head of the sail and not around the rigging.

3. Take care when working on the coach roof. Close the main hatch to avoid falling down the companionway.

4. Loop the halyard round the cleat and pull it tight so the sail is ready to go up but is secure. Don't do this with a wire halyard as it may damage the halyard, the cleat and the mast. Instead, secure the sail with a sail tie.

5. Undo the coils of the mainsheet but keep it jammed tight until the crew has finished working around the boom.

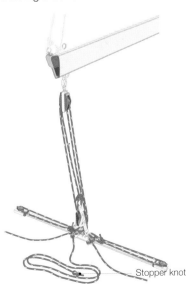

Stopper knot

Jib

1. Attach the tack of the sail to the D ring and hank the sail to the forestay.
2. Clip the halyard to the head of the sail and secure to the pulpit.
3. Tie the sheets to the clew of the sail and to the pulpit.
4. Add a figure-of-eight knot to the end of the sheets.
5. Move the sheet cars on both side decks to the correct position.
6. Secure the sail neatly to the top guardrail.

Head foil

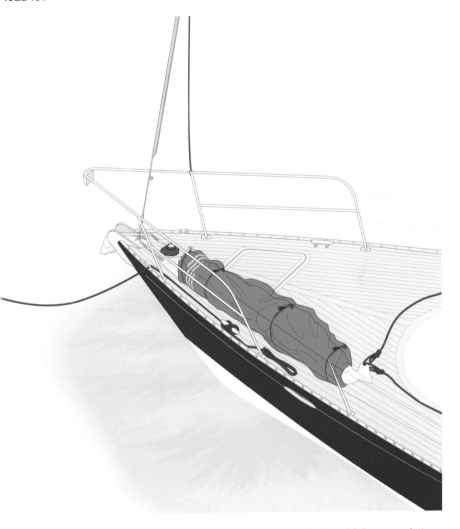

The sail is stowed on deck ready to be fed into the groove on the head foil, secured at the tack, the sheets tied on and then led back to the cockpit ready for use. A roller furling headsail is very easy – just unfurl it when ready.

Hoisting the Mainsail

1. Remove the sail ties.

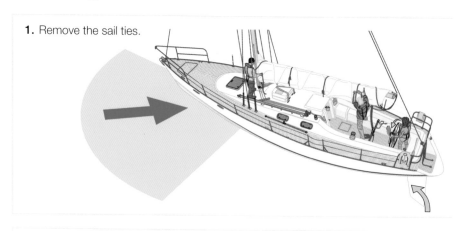

2. Head the boat close to the wind but not straight into it. The mainsail will flap as it is raised and the boom will be to one side of the cockpit, away from the crew winching the halyard.

3. Position the crew in front of the mast or in the cockpit, always clear of the boom.

4. Release the mainsheet and the kicking strap when the crew is clear.

5. Free the main halyard and pull it 'out and down' at the mast, while taking up the slack through an open jammer in the cockpit.

6. Watch the sail for any jams as it goes up. Check that it is flapping all the time. Adjust the halyard tension so that the sail is set correctly.

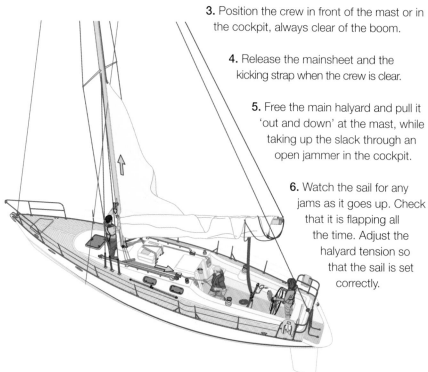

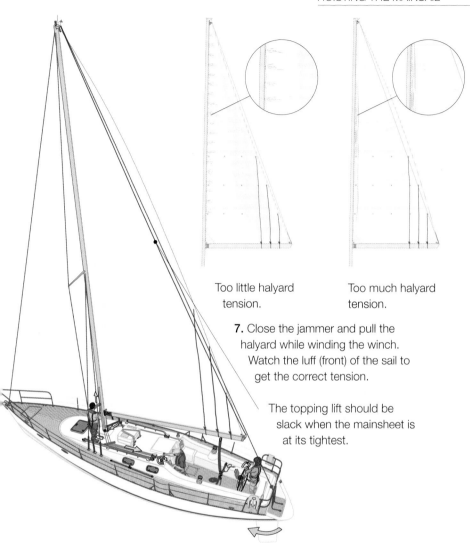

Too little halyard tension.

Too much halyard tension.

7. Close the jammer and pull the halyard while winding the winch. Watch the luff (front) of the sail to get the correct tension.

The topping lift should be slack when the mainsheet is at its tightest.

. Pull in the mainsheet and ease
he topping lift.

. Tighten the kicking strap,
heck the outhaul and stow
he halyard.

0. The helm can now bear away
om the wind and sail.

Hoisting the Jib

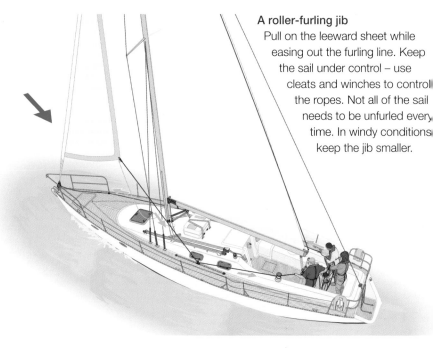

A roller-furling jib
Pull on the leeward sheet while easing out the furling line. Keep the sail under control – use cleats and winches to control the ropes. Not all of the sail needs to be unfurled every time. In windy conditions keep the jib smaller.

A hanked-on foresail
1. Make the sail ready to go. Remove ties and release the halyard.

2. Slacken the sheet.

3. Pull halyard 'out and down' at the mast while taking up the slack through an open jammer in the cockpit.

4. Watch the sail does not snag as it goes up.

5. Close the jammer and pull the halyard while winding the winch. Watch the luff of the sail to get the correct tension. Pull in and winch tight the sheet on the leeward side to the correct tension – and sail!

A loose-luffed jib

1. Feed the head into the luff groove, attach the halyard and release the ties.

Set the halyard tension then pull in the sheets – jib then main – no more than is necessary to stop them flapping.

2. Feed the luff of the sail into the groove while the halyard is slowly pulled to raise the sail. Watch for snags as it goes up and make sure it stays in the pre-feeder.

Now adjust the genoa car position to suit the sail.

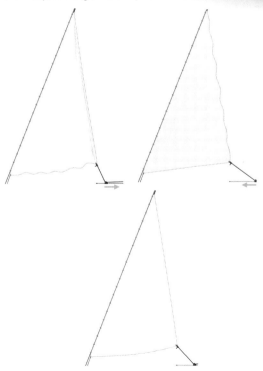

Reefing the Mainsail

TOO MUCH SAIL ON A WINDY DAY

The boat needs to be balanced against the power of the wind. It is normal to reduce the amount of sail progressively as it gets windier. You can reef the mainsail, roll up some of the headsail, change to smaller sails or perform a combination of these techniques. Too much sail:

· Makes the boat difficult to steer straight – the wheel or tiller is too heavy
· Causes the boat to heel (lean over) excessively
· Makes the boat lose speed
· Gives the boat a tendency to broach (heel suddenly and uncontrollably and head towards the wind) in gusts. This can be alarming and sometimes dangerous – it's time to put a reef in.

Trisail

A very small strong sail rigged in very strong winds instead of the main.

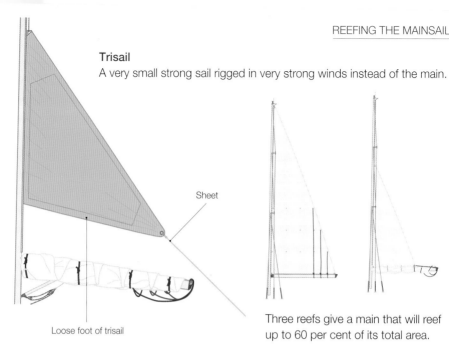

Sheet

Loose foot of trisail

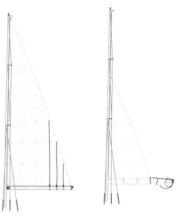

Three reefs give a main that will reef up to 60 per cent of its total area.

Reefing

Reefing is the reduction of the main sail in size. There are several methods of reefing, depending on how a boat is rigged. Slab reefing, shown here, is one of the most common.

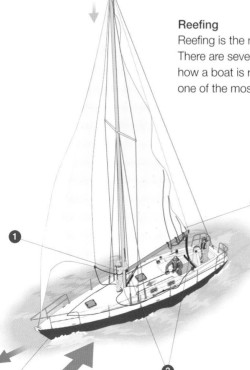

1. Send the crew to the mast on the windward side wearing a harness.

2. Head the boat close to, but not straight into the wind.

3. Ease out the kicking strap then the mainsheet.

4. Pull up on the topping lift to raise the boom and de-power the sail.

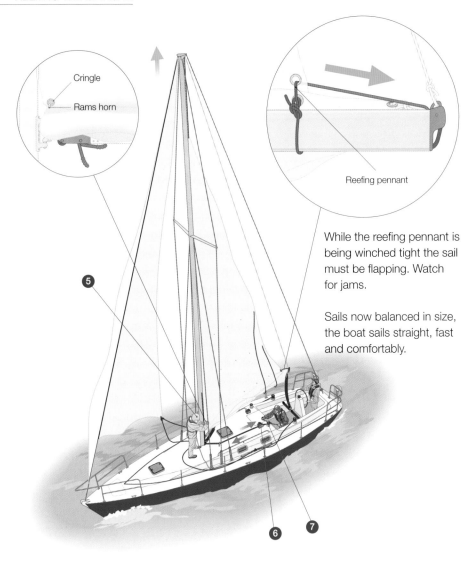

Cringle

Rams horn

Reefing pennant

While the reefing pennant is being winched tight the sail must be flapping. Watch for jams.

Sails now balanced in size, the boat sails straight, fast and comfortably.

5. With the mainsail flapping, lift the jammer and ease the halyard. Pull the sail down and hook the cringle in the luff of the sail over the ram's horn and hold in position.

6. Shut the jammer and winch the halyard tight again.

7. Winch the reefing pennant tight.

8. Ease the topping lift and pull in the mainsheet and kicking strap.

9. Pull in the slack in the other reefing pennant and tidy all lines.

10. Use reef knots to tidy the sail onto the boom with the sail ties – but not tight enough to strain the sail.

Reef knot

Changing the Headsail

Having reefed the mainsail, it is normal to reduce the size of the jib to keep that all-important 'balance'.

Roller-furling jib

This one is easy to do. Pull on the furling line to rotate the forestay and furl the jib. Ease out the sheet, keeping it under tension to ensure a smooth furl.

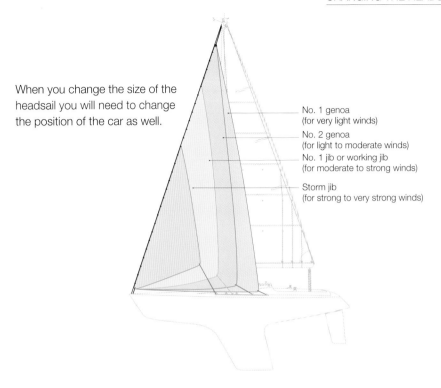

When you change the size of the headsail you will need to change the position of the car as well.

No. 1 genoa
(for very light winds)

No. 2 genoa
(for light to moderate winds)

No. 1 jib or working jib
(for moderate to strong winds)

Storm jib
(for strong to very strong winds)

Hanked-on jib

Here you change to a smaller sail, no. 1 to a 2 or 3. You can prepare the new headsail for hoisting before you drop the old one. With foil sails you have to remove the old one first, unless you have a twin-groove track.

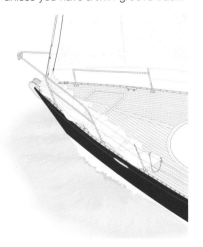

Dropping the headsail

1. Ease out the halyard.

2. Pull down on the luff of the sail. Keep some tension on the jib sheet so neither the sail nor the sheet goes over the side.

Large headsails may need two people on the foredeck to control the sail.

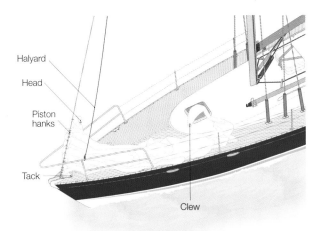

Halyard

Head

Piston
hanks

Tack

Clew

3. Remove the halyard from the sail and clip it into the pulpit. Re-tension the halyard.

4. Pull the sail back and roll it so it can be tied to the guardrail to use again.

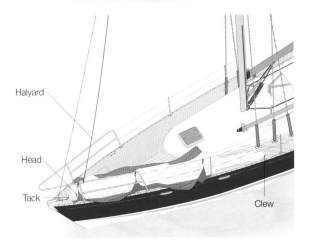

Halyard

Head

Tack

Clew

5. If not required again, fold it from the clew forward. Remove the hanks and stuff it into its sailbag.

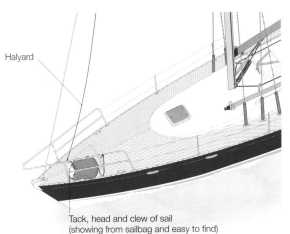

Halyard

Tack, head and clew of sail
(showing from sailbag and easy to find)

6. Keep the bag and sail tied in place.

7. Coil up and tidy away all sheets and the halyard.

Stowing the Mainsail

Bagging the mainsail

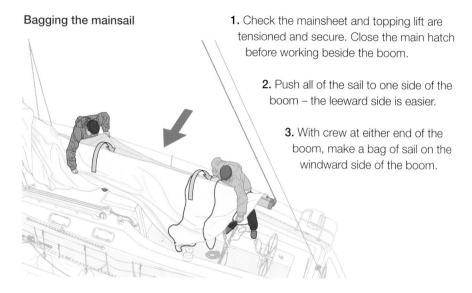

1. Check the mainsheet and topping lift are tensioned and secure. Close the main hatch before working beside the boom.

2. Push all of the sail to one side of the boom – the leeward side is easier.

3. With crew at either end of the boom, make a bag of sail on the windward side of the boom.

4. Working together, grab folds of sail. Pull towards the back of the boom and push them into the bag. Lift in the slack reefing pennants too.

5. Keep working until all the sail is in the bag. Roll the bag tight and lift it onto the top of the boom. Secure with sail ties or lashings.

6. Bagging works well for short-term storage.

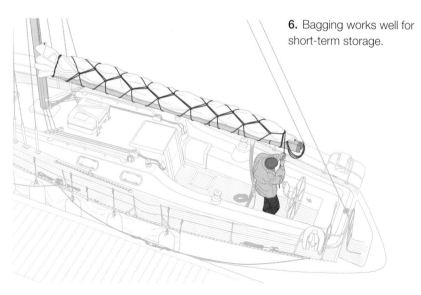

Flaking the mainsail

1. Push all of the sail to one side of the boom – the leeward side is easier.

2. With crew at either end of the boom, flake the sail from one side of the boom to the other in even-sized folds. Keep pulling the sail towards the stern to keep it flat.

3. Hold the sail in place with the sail ties. Secure the head of the sail.

4. Flaking is usually better for longer term storage as it means fewer creases.

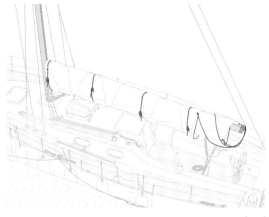

Stowing the Jib

Flaking the jib

1. Stretch out the foot of the sail on the pontoon alongside the boat. Keep the head on the boat.

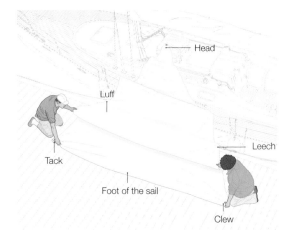

2. Kneel on the sail and, working together, grab a fold of sail and place it on top of the foot.

3. Keep the foot stretched and keep flaking towards the head of the sail.

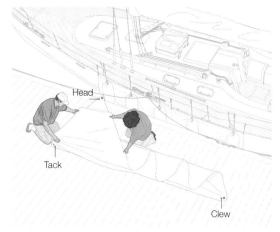

4. Fold the sail from the clew towards the luff.

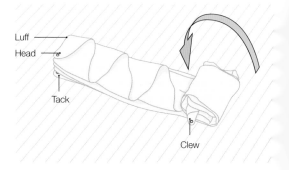

Keep the corners uppermost in the bag so they are easy to find – especially the tack.

To fit long sail bags, make an 'S' fold to keep the head, tack and clew at the ends of the bag.

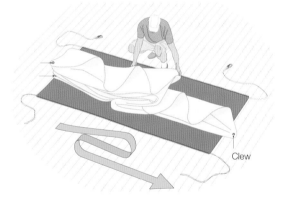

Clew

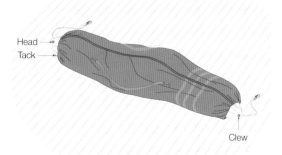

Head
Tack

Clew

How and Why Sails Work

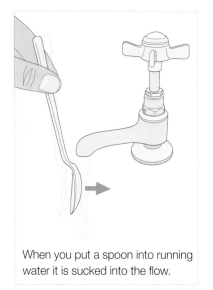

When you put a spoon into running water it is sucked into the flow.

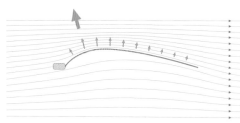

Air on the sail behaves in a similar way, so as the flow of air over the sail produces pressure changes this gives lift and increases the speed of the wind blowing over the upper surface, like an aircraft's wing.

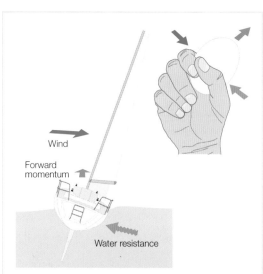

Wind

Forward momentum

Water resistance

A combination of a sideways force from the sail and opposite resistance from the water provided by the boat's underwater shape and the keel help push it forward rather than just sideways – like squeezing a bar of wet soap.

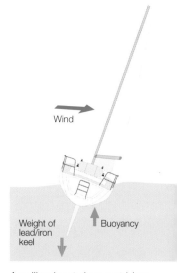

Wind

Weight of lead/iron keel

Buoyancy

A sailing boat does not blow over as the force of the wind is counterbalanced by its own weight and buoyancy.

Wind Awareness

In order to develop a good sense of wind awareness there are numerous ways of identifying the wind direction. Turning your head so you can feel the wind directly on your face is one. On the boat there will be flags or wind indicators, and outside the boat the direction of the waves can be used, or, if close to land, things such as chimney smoke and trees can help.

Points of Sailing

A modern yacht will sail at almost any angle to the wind apart from the 'no-go' zone – an angle roughly 45° each side of the wind direction.

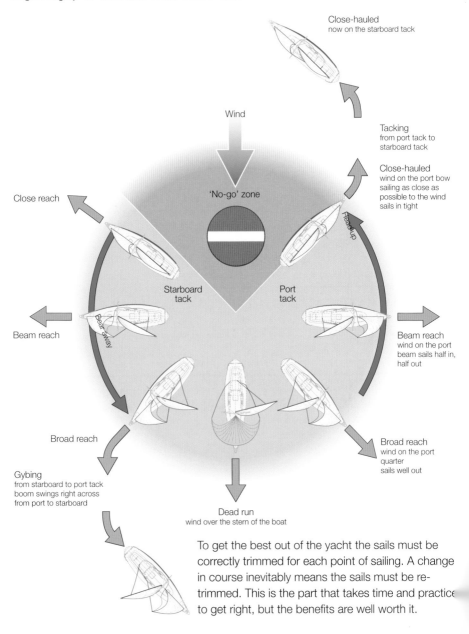

Close-hauled
now on the starboard tack

Wind

Tacking
from port tack to
starboard tack

Close-hauled
wind on the port bow
sailing as close as
possible to the wind
sails in tight

Close reach

'No-go' zone

Head-up

Starboard
tack

Port
tack

Beam reach

Bear away

Beam reach
wind on the port
beam sails half in,
half out

Broad reach

Broad reach
wind on the port
quarter
sails well out

Gybing
from starboard to port tack
boom swings right across
from port to starboard

Dead run
wind over the stern of the boat

To get the best out of the yacht the sails must be correctly trimmed for each point of sailing. A change in course inevitably means the sails must be re-trimmed. This is the part that takes time and practice to get right, but the benefits are well worth it.

Sailing on the Wind

When the sails on the boat are set correctly the boat will feel alive and well balanced.

Close-hauled – correct course

The waves are an excellent guide to where the wind is coming from.

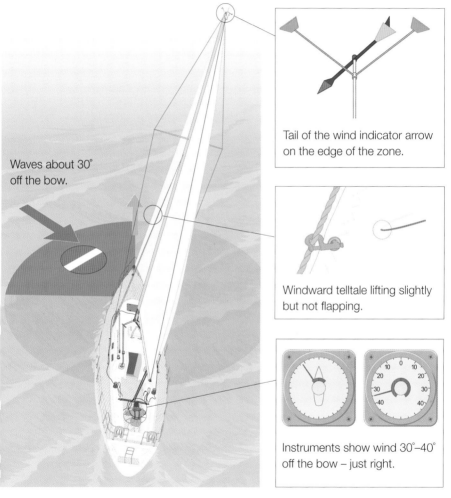

Waves about 30° off the bow.

Tail of the wind indicator arrow on the edge of the zone.

Windward telltale lifting slightly but not flapping.

Instruments show wind 30°–40° off the bow – just right.

- Sails in tight
- Helm not too heavy, with a small amount of weather helm. This is where the heel of the yacht and the pressure from the sails creates feel on the helm, making it easier to steer the yacht.
- A good helmsman will use a combination of all these factors to maintain a good course and keep the yacht 'in the groove'.

Too close to the wind

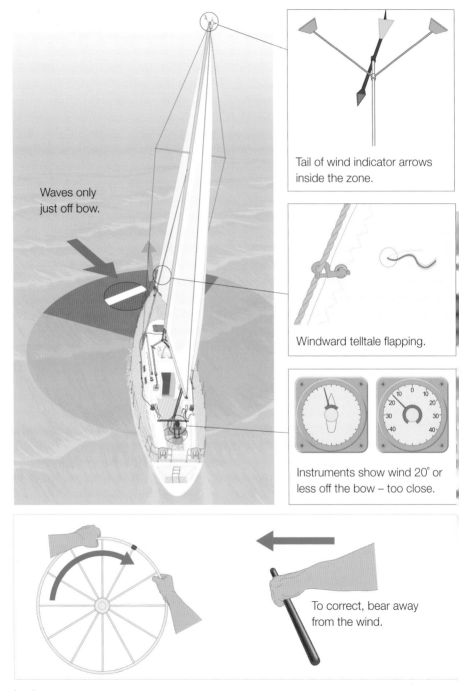

Tail of wind indicator arrows inside the zone.

Waves only just off bow.

Windward telltale flapping.

Instruments show wind 20° or less off the bow – too close.

To correct, bear away from the wind.

Too far off the wind

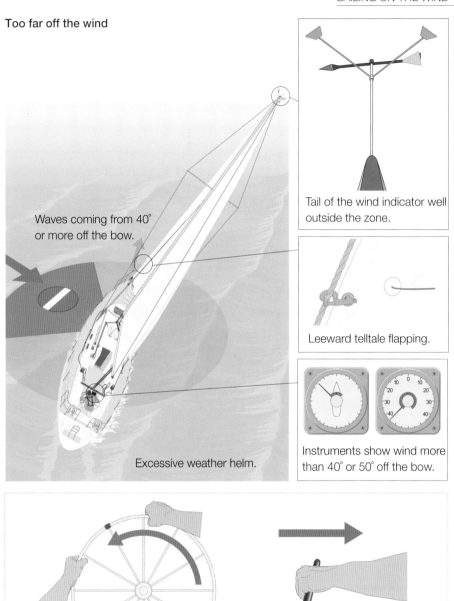

Tail of the wind indicator well outside the zone.

Waves coming from 40° or more off the bow.

Leeward telltale flapping.

Excessive weather helm.

Instruments show wind more than 40° or 50° off the bow.

To correct, head up close to the wind.

Sailing Upwind – Tacking

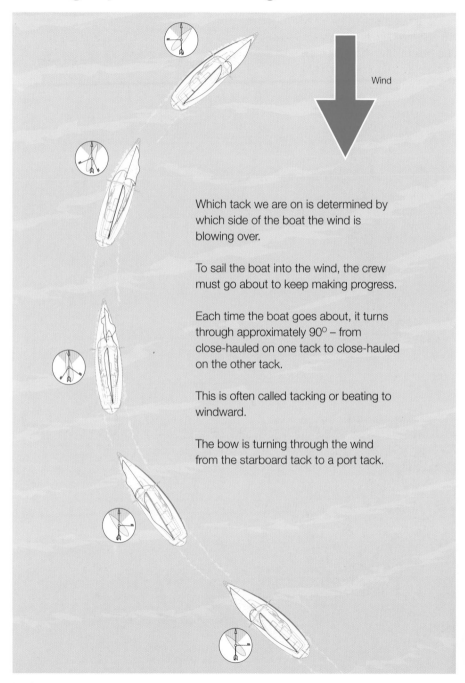

Wind

Which tack we are on is determined by which side of the boat the wind is blowing over.

To sail the boat into the wind, the crew must go about to keep making progress.

Each time the boat goes about, it turns through approximately 90° – from close-hauled on one tack to close-hauled on the other tack.

This is often called tacking or beating to windward.

The bow is turning through the wind from the starboard tack to a port tack.

Going About

Going about is turning the boat's bow through the wind from close-hauled on one tack to close-hauled on the other. Remember to look around before changing course.

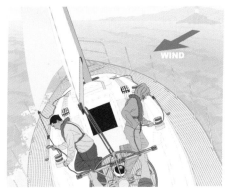

1. Look around. Helmsman calls "Ready about". Crew prepares the jib sheets.

2. When all ready, the helmsman calls "helm to lee" and turns the bow towards the wind.

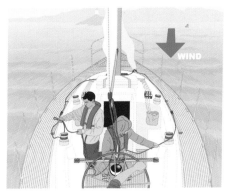

3. Head to wind – the crew let fly the old jib sheet, making sure it can run free, and quickly pulls in the new one, ready to winch it in.

4. The sails have changed sides on to port tack and begin to fill. Centre the helm.

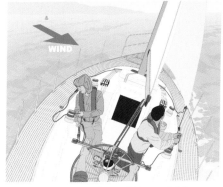

5. Crew fine tunes the sail trim and tidies up.

Sail Trim on a Reach

On each point of sail there are various indicators which tell you how well the sails are working. You can then adjust the sails in or out to improve performance.

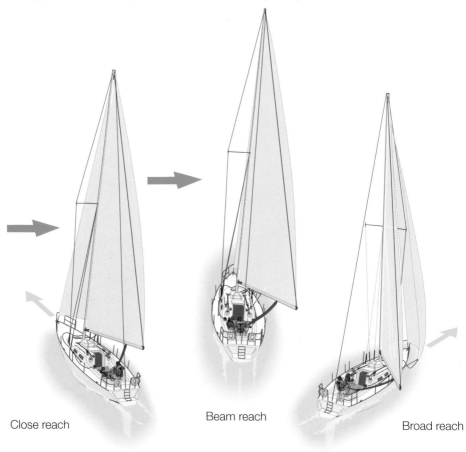

Close reach

Beam reach

Broad reach

Close reach on
the port tack.
Wind coming over
the port bow.

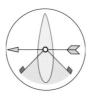

Beam reach on
the port tack.
Wind coming over
the port beam.

Broad reach on
the port tack.
Wind coming over
the port quarter.

The jib telltales have a story for you.

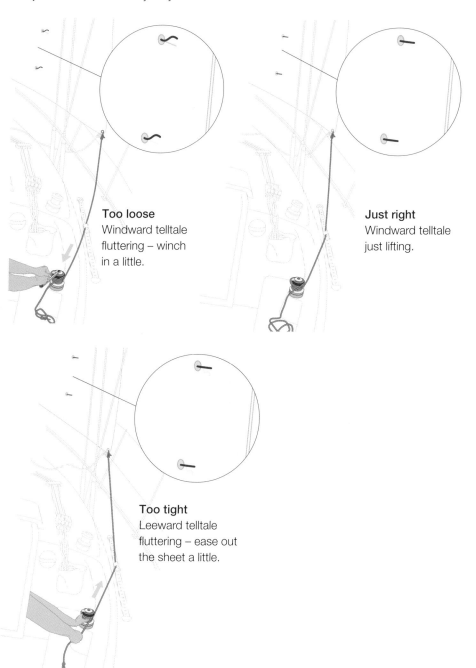

Too loose
Windward telltale
fluttering – winch
in a little.

Just right
Windward telltale
just lifting.

Too tight
Leeward telltale
fluttering – ease out
the sheet a little.

Sailing Downwind

Sailing with the wind abaft or behind the beam of the boat. Here the telltales are less helpful but the windex is a great aid.

Broad reach on the starboard tack. Windex arrow on the edge of the quadrant zone and the wind coming over the starboard quarter.

Windex arrow in the middle of the quadrant zone. Wind directly astern risking an accidental gybe.

Windex arrow out of the quadrant zone. Wind off the starboard beam. Time for the boat to bear away to maintain a broad reach.

Windex arrow on edge of the zone.

Windex arrow in the zone.

Wind indicator arrow too close to the beam.

Headsail 'collapses'

Wind on the quarter – both sails working on a broad reach.

This boat has borne away too much, losing speed and risking an accidental gybe – head up.

This boat can bear away safely to achieve a broad reach.

An accidental gybe

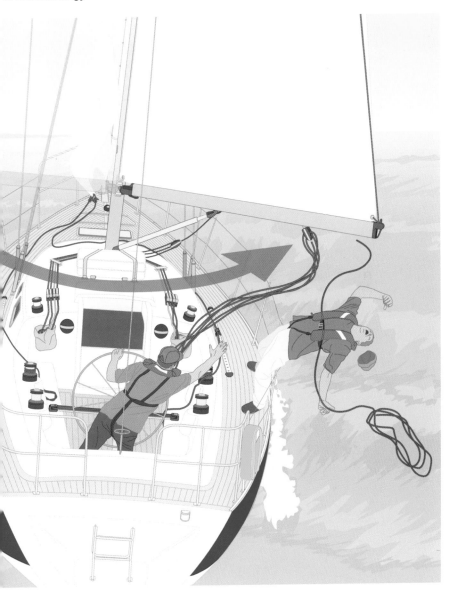

If the boom moves suddenly and unexpectedly across the boat it can be dangerous. If, when the wind is coming from behind the boat, the helmsman bears away too much, the jib will collapse because it is in the wind shadow of the mainsail. This indicates that you are close to a gybe. Head up a little closer to the wind to avoid an accidental gybe and get the jib working again.

Poled-out headsail

When the wind is dead astern it can be simpler to pole out the head sail so it is not blanketed by the main sail.

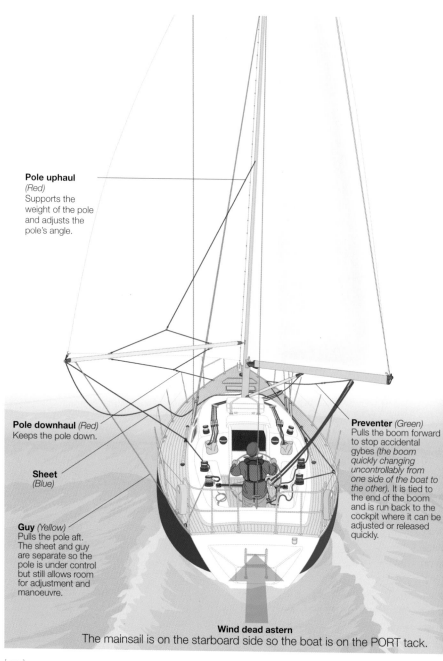

Pole uphaul
(Red)
Supports the weight of the pole and adjusts the pole's angle.

Pole downhaul *(Red)*
Keeps the pole down.

Sheet
(Blue)

Guy *(Yellow)*
Pulls the pole aft. The sheet and guy are separate so the pole is under control but still allows room for adjustment and manoeuvre.

Preventer *(Green)*
Pulls the boom forward to stop accidental gybes *(the boom quickly changing uncontrollably from one side of the boat to the other)*. It is tied to the end of the boom and is run back to the cockpit where it can be adjusted or released quickly.

Wind dead astern
The mainsail is on the starboard side so the boat is on the PORT tack.

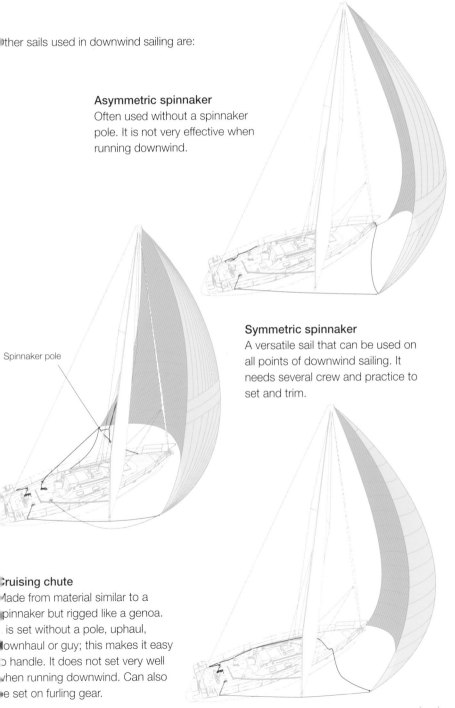

ther sails used in downwind sailing are:

Asymmetric spinnaker
Often used without a spinnaker
pole. It is not very effective when
running downwind.

Spinnaker pole

Symmetric spinnaker
A versatile sail that can be used on
all points of downwind sailing. It
needs several crew and practice to
set and trim.

Cruising chute
Made from material similar to a
spinnaker but rigged like a genoa.
 is set without a pole, uphaul,
downhaul or guy; this makes it easy
o handle. It does not set very well
when running downwind. Can also
e set on furling gear.

Gybing under Control

When sailing downwind it is often faster overall and safer to zigzag downwind, sailing a series of broad reaches using a controlled gybe.

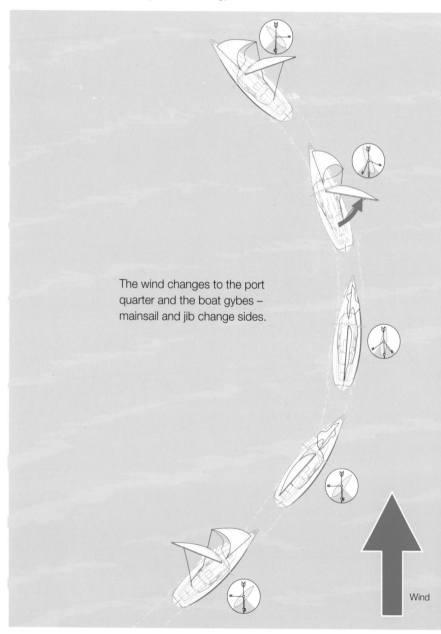

The wind changes to the port quarter and the boat gybes – mainsail and jib change sides.

Wind

A controlled gybe from a broad reach or a run is a safe procedure.

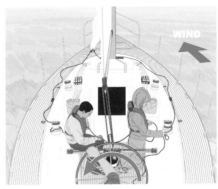

The helmsman starts the sequence by calling "stand by to gybe". If a gybe preventer is rigged it is released. The crew sheets the mainsail in and prepares the headsail sheets.

When the main is in the middle the helmsman turns the wheel to gybe.

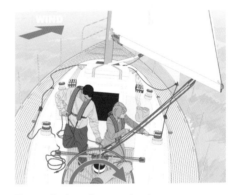

The main flips across. Sheet the jib in on the same side as the main and when it is under tension release the other sheet.

The mainsheet is eased out.

The crew make final adjustments to the sail trim. The gybe preventer may be rigged again.

Steering

When a yacht is turned it will pivot about the keel. The rudder is moved by pushing or pulling on the tiller or turning the wheel.

Tiller steering
Push the tiller to port to turn the boat to starboard and vice-versa.

Wheel steering
Turn the wheel the same way you want to turn the boat.

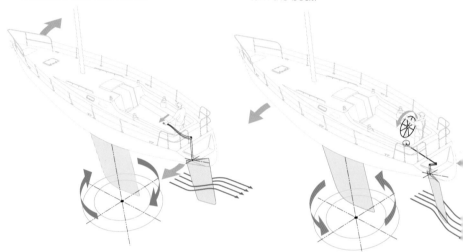

If you are off course, correcting takes practice. Make a small alteration, straighten up and check the effect on the compass. Average out the course – if you have consistently sailed on one side of the course, compensate by sailing an equal amount on the other.

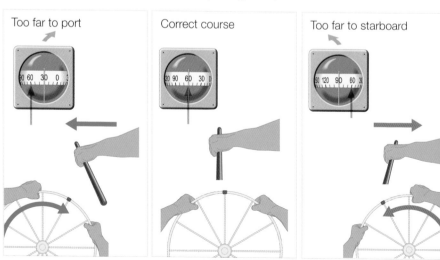

| Too far to port | Correct course | Too far to starboard |

Steering a Steady Course

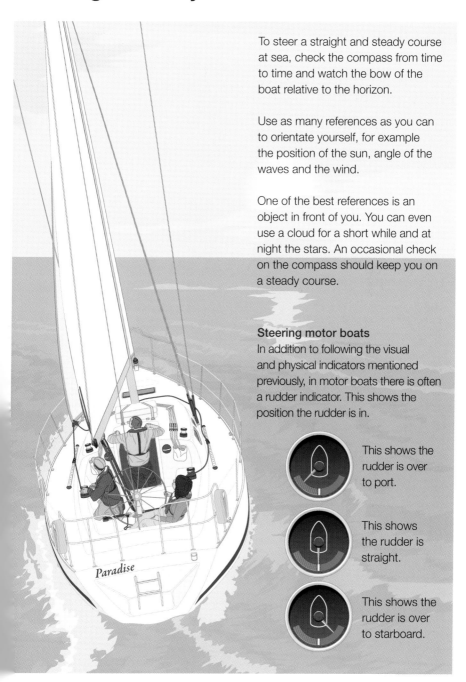

To steer a straight and steady course at sea, check the compass from time to time and watch the bow of the boat relative to the horizon.

Use as many references as you can to orientate yourself, for example the position of the sun, angle of the waves and the wind.

One of the best references is an object in front of you. You can even use a cloud for a short while and at night the stars. An occasional check on the compass should keep you on a steady course.

Steering motor boats
In addition to following the visual and physical indicators mentioned previously, in motor boats there is often a rudder indicator. This shows the position the rudder is in.

This shows the rudder is over to port.

This shows the rudder is straight.

This shows the rudder is over to starboard.

Paradise

Coming Alongside in a Marina

1. The skipper may call the marina on the VHF to arrange a berth.

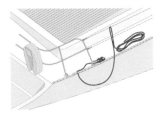

Lead the warp from the cleat, through the fairlead, forward to the side deck ready for the crew to take ashore.

2. Prepare the fenders and mooring lines on both sides of the boat to be ready for any change of plan.

3. Position the crew amidships ready to step ashore.

A crew member stationed near the bow can if necessary protect the boat with a fender and call the distance off to the helmsman.

4. Step ashore with the lines in a neat coil. Don't jump.

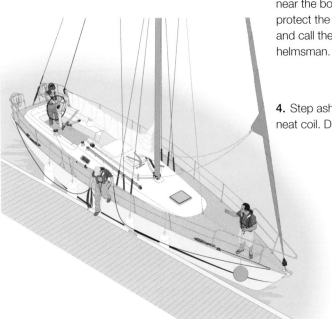

5. Take a turn round a cleat and be ready to pull in or ease out if necessary.

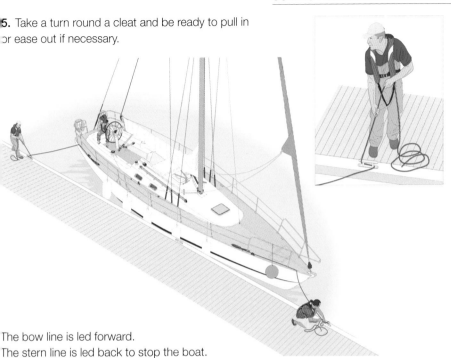

The bow line is led forward.
The stern line is led back to stop the boat.

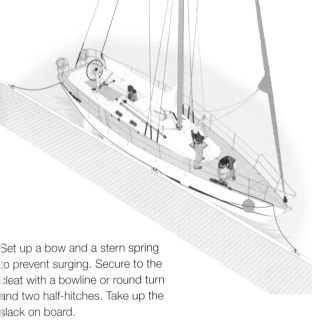

Set up a bow and a stern spring to prevent surging. Secure to the cleat with a bowline or round turn and two half-hitches. Take up the slack on board.

Bowline looped round the cleat – easy to release but will not come off accidentally.

Coming alongside in motor boats or high-sided boats

Before making the approach, the skipper will brief the crew to ready the lines and fenders and to be in position at either the bow or stern ready to throw the line around the cleat when signalled.

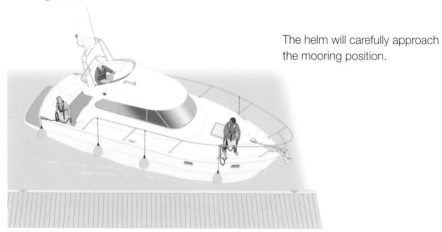

The helm will carefully approach the mooring position.

When the skipper signals to do so, throw the line around the cleat. Whether the bow or the stern line goes on first will be determined by the conditions.

Once both lines are on, these can be tightened and a spring may be used

Mooring Alongside another Boat

1. If possible, talk first with the crew of the other boat – are they about to leave? If not...

2. Moor to the other vessel using fenders rigged higher than normal, bow line, stern line and springs. Then lead long lines ashore so that all the weight of your boat is not hanging on the other boat's lines.

Check the boats are parallel so you don't end up bows in.

3. Make sure the lines are long enough to allow for any rise and fall of tide.

A fender board can be rigged to stop any projections in the wall damaging the hull.

Leaving a Berth

Alongside berth

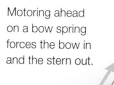

Motoring ahead
on a bow spring
forces the bow in
and the stern out.

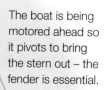

The boat is being
motored ahead so
it pivots to bring
the stern out – the
fender is essential.

Get the lines ready to slip.
Remember the short end of the
line should be on top of the cleat.

A slip line can be quickly released
and quickly pulled on board.

This slip line must be carefully
prepared to slip when the skipper
reverses away.

Alongside berth in motor boats

Before starting to leave the berth, the skipper will brief the crew about what is going to
happen and what role they are going to play. Like coming alongside, the crew will need to
be in position at the bow or the stern with the lines ready to be slipped when signalled by
the skipper.

Leaving a raft

Crew ready to pull the bow line from the boat to the shore.

Yacht preparing to leave, shore lines removed.

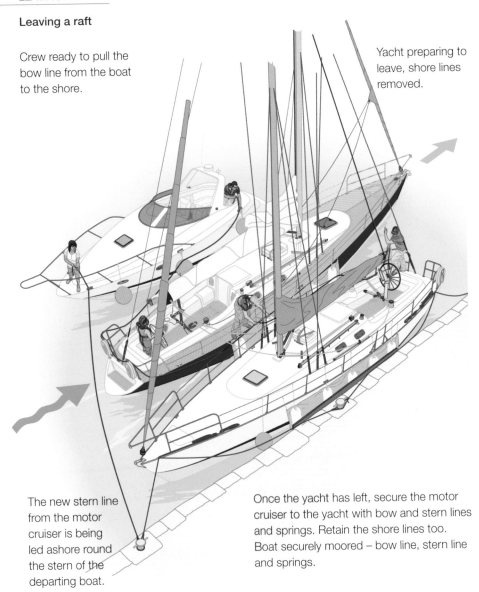

The new stern line from the motor cruiser is being led ashore round the stern of the departing boat.

Once the yacht has left, secure the motor cruiser to the yacht with bow and stern lines and springs. Retain the shore lines too. Boat securely moored – bow line, stern line and springs.

Picking up a Mooring

Mooring buoys are excellent for an overnight or longer stay. Check with the mooring owner first where possible.

1. The helm will need to approach the mooring in the same direction as the other moored yachts are lying – usually into the tidal stream or head to the wind if no tide.

2. Point towards the buoy and call the distances – the helmsman probably can't see the buoy.

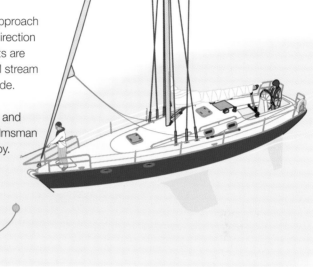

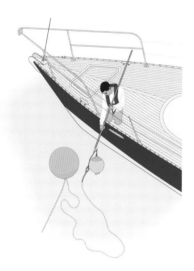

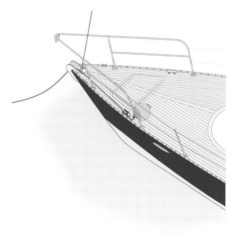

3. Lift the pick-up buoy to catch the mooring loop.

4. Drop the loop over the cleat and secure it in position. Make sure it is led through the bow roller.

When there is no pick-up buoy or rope

Be ready to lean down to the buoy.

1. One crew catches the buoy by the ring whilst the other attaches a mooring warp.

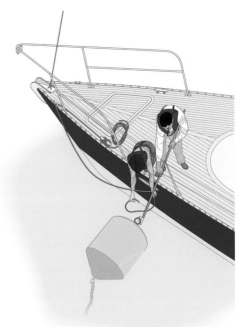

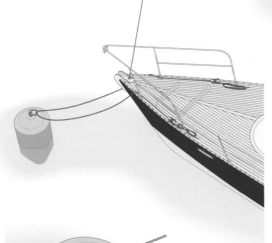

2. For a brief stay, rig a slip line through the ring on the buoy using a mooring warp.

3. For an overnight stop, secure with a round turn and a bowline.

Picking up a mooring in a motor boat

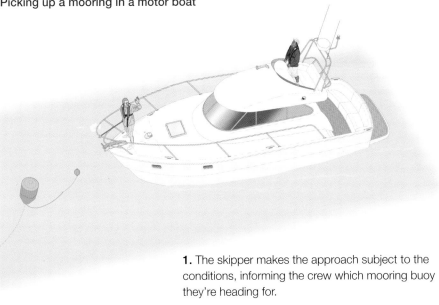

1. The skipper makes the approach subject to the conditions, informing the crew which mooring buoy they're heading for.

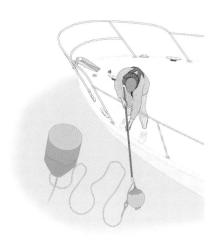

2. Crew member stands ready to collect the pick-up buoy (probably with a boat hook on a larger vessel.)

3. If there is no pick-up buoy, the crew members work together to pass a line through the mooring ring.

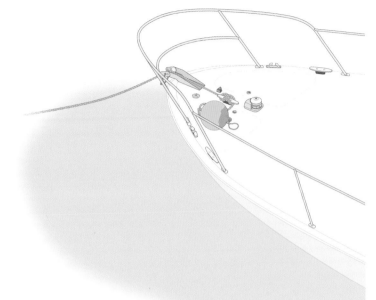

4. Crew attaches pick-up line to cleat on the bow.

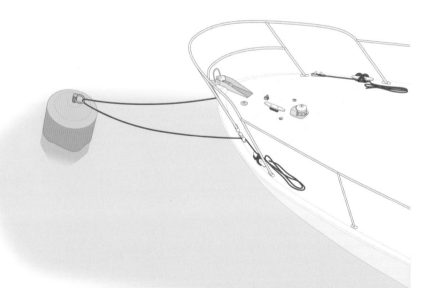

5. Where there is no pick-up buoy, the mooring loop is secured to the cleat either side of the bow. Extra lines may be used if staying for a prolonged period.

Anchoring

Anchoring is a great free way to spend some time. Make sure that there will be sufficient water at low tide.

Dropping anchor

If necessary, secure a tripping line to the anchor and lead it so it cannot get caught up when the anchor is put down.

Secure to the cleat. Make sure that the end of the chain that goes back into the locker is on top of the cleat.

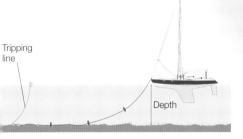

Tripping line

Depth

Flake out the correct length of chain onto the deck (usually four times the maximum depth of water).

Weighing anchor

If the anchor is fouled use the trip line to pull it free.

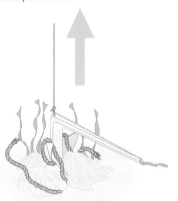

Pull up the chain to raise the anchor – bend your knees, not your back.

The skipper will motor the boat gently forward to take the weight off the chain.

Using a windlass

Once the vessel is in the anchoring position, the skipper will hold the vessel in a stable position.

The crew will get ready for anchoring by opening and securing the inspection hatch.

The crew will then release the safety catch securing the anchor chain to the windlass.

On the signal from the skipper, the crew will feed out the chain using the hand or foot control. As the anchor is dropped, the crew monitors the chain inside the hatch to watch for tangles.

When weighing anchor, it's important to monitor that the incoming chain doesn't tangle inside the hatch. Once the chain is fully retracted, attach the safety catch.

Rules of the Road

SAILING VESSELS
Port/starboard situation

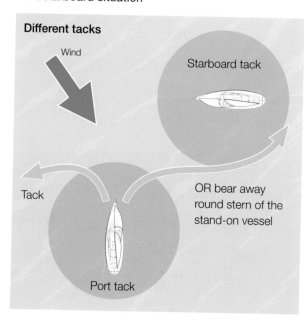

Different tacks

Wind

Starboard tack

Tack

OR bear away
round stern of the
stand-on vessel

Port tack

Port tack always
keeps clear whatever
the point of sailing.

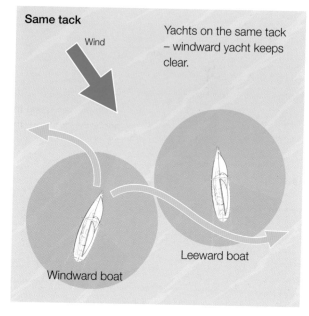

Same tack

Wind

Yachts on the same tack
– windward yacht keeps
clear.

Leeward boat

Windward boat

Motor vessels/yachts under power

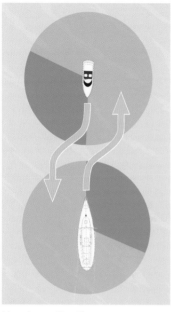

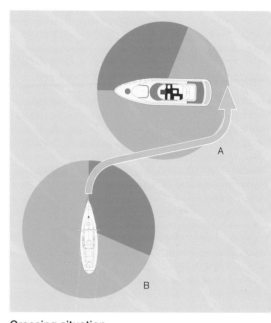

Head-on situation
Both vessels turn to starboard.

Crossing situation
A is on the starboard side of B. B gives way to A.

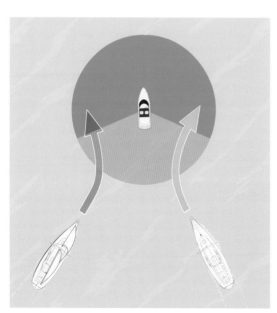

Overtaking situation
Stand-on vessel must keep a steady course and speed.

Any vessel in this sector – power or sail – must give way to the vessel being overtaken.

Give-way vessels must make their intentions clear by making an early, bold alteration of course.

How can we tell if a risk of collision exists?

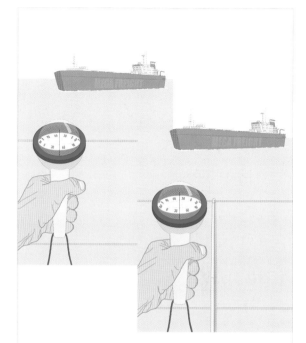

1. While on a steady course, take a bearing of the ship or line it up with a part of your boat such as a stanchion or stay.

2. If the bearing of the ship changes or moves in relation to your stanchion there will not be a collision.

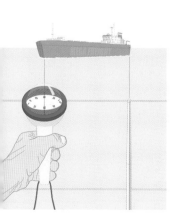

If the bearing stays steady or the ship remains lined up with your stanchion then a risk of collision exists.

Keeping a Lookout

Keeping a good lookout is a fundamental part of sailing. Remember that you travel slower than many other craft so you need to watch all round. Be especially vigilant behind as other craft may catch you up very quickly.

DAY: look out for:

- Racing marks and fishing pots.
- Fast approaching sea-cats and ships.
- Rubbish in the water.
- Yachts on a closing course
    - Who is the give-way vessel?
- Where is the shipping lane?
    - Are we out of the way of the ships?
    - Where are the buoys?
    - What is the depth on the echo sounder? Too shallow and we might go aground. Too deep and we could be in the shipping channel.
- Monitor the VHF for information.

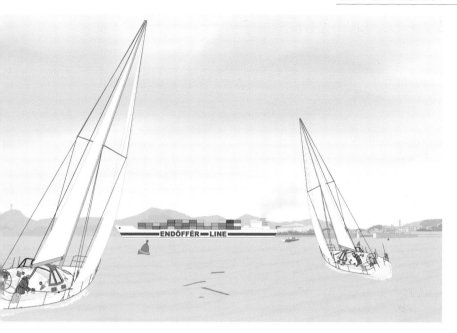

NIGHT: look out for:

At night, ensure your vessel is lit correctly, and watch under the head sail for fast-approaching craft. Look up as well – large ship lights are much higher than you.

- · Lights
    - Flashing lights are navigation marks – buoys, beacons, lighthouses.
    - Fixed lights at sea are boats.
    - Near harbours it can be difficult to spot vessels or buoys because of the background lights.
- · All crew should clip on.
- · Watch for unlit buoys and flotsam.
- · Do not use white lights down below – it ruins everyone's night vision.
- · Watch for small boats moving, not just ships.

Watch Keeping

You will probably keep watches if you are sailing for longer than a normal day.

A good skipper doesn't wait until nightfall to start the rota when everyone is already tired. They will share out duties, make sure the crew members keep warm and dry and have suitable meals.

A good watch-keeping rota will prevent a sole crew being alone, tired and cold at night.

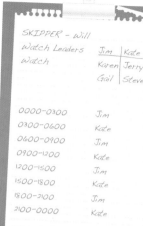

SKIPPER – Will

Watch Leaders	Jim	Kate
Watch	Karen	Jerry
	Gail	Steve

0000–0300	Jim
0300–0600	Kate
0600–0900	Jim
0900–1200	Kate
1200–1500	Jim
1500–1800	Kate
1800–2100	Jim
2100–0000	Kate

When you are on watch make sure you look all around you and behind the jib periodically.

When you are coming on watch arrive in good time.

Sailing Manners and Nautical Customs

Learning the customs and manners of seafaring folk is good fun and helps you make friends.

In harbour, raise the ensign at 0800hrs (summer) and 0900hrs (winter). Lower the ensign at sunset or 2100hrs local time, whichever is earlier.

The ensign is flown day and night at sea.

Before mooring alongside, ask. Then walk round by the foredeck to go ashore – quietly. Don't wake up other crew when you return.

Do not use the heads in the marina unless you have holding tanks.

Do not throw foodstuff over the side, even if it is biodegradable.

Do not dump rubbish in the sea.

Do not pump or spill oil, diesel, paint or other chemicals into the water.

Using the Dinghy

Every year more accidents happen to crews going ashore by dinghy than at any other time, so:

Wear lifejackets.
Do not overload the boat – make two trips if necessary.

Carry oars, the dinghy pump and spare fuel for the outboard, just in case.

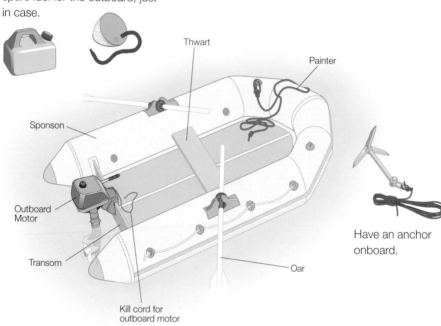

Thwart

Painter

Sponson

Outboard
Motor

Transom

Oar

Have an anchor
onboard.

Kill cord for
outboard motor

Carry a box containing:
· Tools.
· Bailer.
· Flares.
· Torch.
· Sparkplug.
· Hand-held VHF.

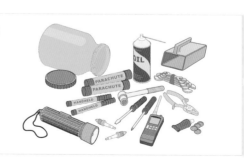

Load the dinghy evenly.

Wear lifejackets and do not overload the boat.

Secure dinghy and unload provisions. Climb on and off the boat with care

Ship the oars and glide alongside slowly and make fast to the jetty before loading

If rowing in a strong tidal stream 'crab' across by heading the bow up into the flow

Make two or three trips in the dinghy instead of one overloaded journey. It will only take an extra few minutes and be safer

Climb in and out with care.

Personal Comfort

Clothing has dramatically changed in recent years and there is no need to get cold or too hot. It is never the weather – just the clothes you are wearing.

It is best to avoid all cotton materials under your waterproofs. Cotton retains the sweat and can make you feel cold.

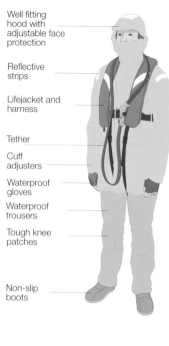

Well fitting hood with adjustable face protection

Reflective strips

Lifejacket and harness

Tether

Cuff adjusters

Waterproof gloves

Waterproof trousers

Tough knee patches

Non-slip boots

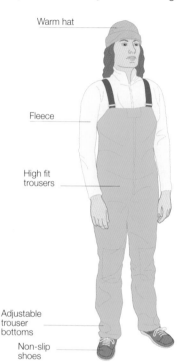

Warm hat

Fleece

High fit trousers

Adjustable trouser bottoms

Non-slip shoes

Use a hat, sunglasses and sunscreen for protection from the sun.

Keep warm.

Drink water to avoid dehydration.

To reduce sea sickness avoid alcohol and fatty foods before you sail. Take anti-sea sickness medicine.

Personal Safety

Lifejackets
Personal safety equipment has also improved in fit and comfort. It is now both easy and unobtrusive to wear.

A modern gas-inflated lifejacket combined with a harness which can be auto-inflating. Use the crotch straps.

A buoyancy aid is better for dinghy sailing.

A lifejacket with integral buoyancy will give support to a conscious casualty who is able to swim.

Extra buoyancy can be added by blowing into the valve.

Children need special jackets to fit them.

Lifejackets that are too big or loose do not provide support in the water and are dangerous. Use crotch straps to keep the jacket down.

Harnesses
Adjust a harness to fit you properly. It must fit tightly to be effective.

Clip onto the jackstay on the windward or 'uphill' side of the vessel before leaving the cockpit.

Clip onto:
- Jackstays.
- D rings.
- Shrouds and stays.

Don't clip onto:
- Ropes.
- Guardrails or anything else.

Man Overboard – Actions to be Taken

1. Shout "man overboard". Point at the casualty in the water.

2. Throw a lifebelt and danbuoy.

3. Don't take your eyes off them and keep pointing.

4. The skipper will ask for the jib to be lowered and start the engine. Keep pointing.

5. Prepare a throwing line.

6. The skipper will come alongside, either with the boat pointing into the wind or beam on, whichever is more suitable. You must stop the propeller. Get a line around the casualty. Bring them aboard via the stern or boarding ladder, or use the halyard and winch them on board.

Man overboard retrieval on a motor boat

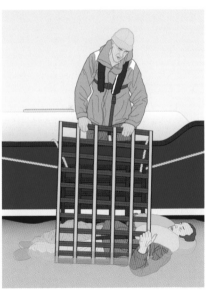

Many motor boats are high sided and, even with a bathing platform and ladder, man overboard recovery is not easy. You will need to collect the man overboard at the area where the side decks are lowest and then attach a line and walk them to your recovery area.

Cold Shock

1. You will most likely gasp for air, then breathe rapidly. You can only hold your breath for a few seconds – protect your airway from waves and spray.

2. Your heart will be working harder, so don't try to swim – just relax!

3. The effects will be at their worst in the first 30 seconds but will have gone within three minutes.

4. Being prepared for this to happen so that you don't panic will greatly reduce the risk.

Fire

Common causes of fire

Solvents/paints stored below.

Cooking fats.

Gas build-up in the bilges.

Faulty wiring.

Smoking below decks.

Extinguishers

Dry powder – don't use on flammable liquids.
CO2 – good for enclosed spaces.
AFFF – foam, good for flammable liquids.

Fire blanket – good for smothering flames.

Fighting the fire

Aim the extinguisher at the base of the flames.

Splashing water from a bucket can be more effective than throwing its entire contents at once.

Fire blankets can be used to smother a galley fire...

...and they are also essential for clothing fires.

Mayday

Only make a Mayday call if there is 'grave and imminent danger' to person or vessel.

Use
- Channel 16.
- High power.

Press button microphone before speaking – release it after the word "over".

VHF/DSC SET – VHF/DSC alert
Press the emergency button for five seconds to send an undesignated distress alert.

Mayday call
"MAYDAY, MAYDAY, MAYDAY
This is yacht Puffin, Puffin, Puffin
Call sign MYFT7 MMSI 232167284"

Mayday message
"MAYDAY
Yacht Puffin Call sign MYFT7 MMSI 232167284
My position is (give latitude and longitude from GPS or bearing and distance FROM a known point)
Nature of distress
Require immediate assistance... (Give number of persons on board)
(Other VITAL information i.e. abandoning to liferaft/have no liferaft)
OVER"

Other Distress Signals

There are lots of other methods of alerting others to your distress.

Buoyant orange smoke
- Daylight use only.
- Use within three miles of rescuer.
- Throw downwind.

Cloud lasts three or four minutes.

Orange smoke is easy for a rescue helicopter to see and gives the wind direction.

Orange hand-held smoke
Cloud lasts about one minute.

Red hand-held flare

· Use day or night.
· Use within three miles of rescuer

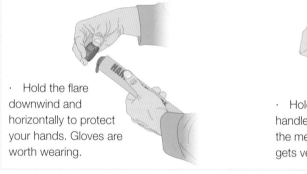

· Hold the flare downwind and horizontally to protect your hands. Gloves are worth wearing.

· Hold by the handle only – the metal casing gets very hot.

Red parachute rocket
Read the instructions on flares and check they are in date.
Remove cap and prepare to fire downwind.

Do not use if a rescue helicopter is nearby.

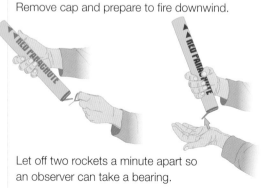

Let off two rockets a minute apart so an observer can take a bearing.

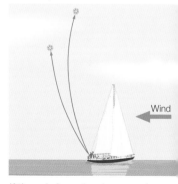

If there is low cloud cover, aim further downwind.

Abandoning to the Liferaft

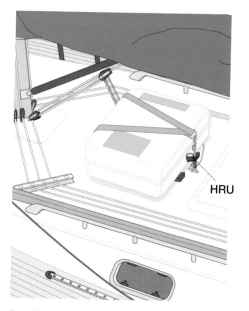

HRU

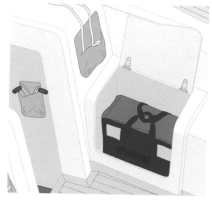

If stowed in a locker it can be a valise style. Do not stow equipment on top of it.

The liferaft is a key item in the boat's safety equipment. If stowed on deck it should be in a GRP canister. Do not use it as a seat! With an HRU (Hydrostatic Release Unit) it will deploy automatically if the boat sinks. Only abandon to the liferaft if there is no hope of saving the vessel. If possible, stay with the boat.

1. Get all the crew ready in their lifejackets. Send a Mayday.

2. Check the painter is tied on, especially if it is stowed in a locker.

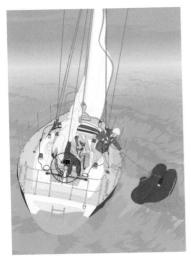

5. Get a heavy adult into the liferaft first for stability.

3. Launch the liferaft on the leeward side.

4. Pull on the painter to inflate the liferaft.

6. Get the crew to climb in, staying dry, if possible. Do not jump into the water.

7. Take extra things if you can – water, carbohydrate foods, first aid kit, warm clothes, sleeping bags, TPA (thermal protection aid).

8. Cut the painter and stream the drogue to increase the stability and reduce drift. Bail out any water. Close the door to preserve warmth and keep the sea out. Take anti-seasickness tablets!

Living Aboard the Boat

Even a reasonable-sized yacht is much smaller than most homes, so you need to adapt to a very different environment.

Think carefully about the gear that you will need and pack it in a soft waterproof bag.

This is more suitable for a cruise liner than a cruising yacht.

Turn off taps to save water.

Switch off lights to save power and not dazzle the crew on deck at night.

Clean as you go!

Don't leave the gas while it is lit. Turn off after use.

Turn off at the tap away from the cooker when finished.

Turn off at the gas bottle when not in use.

Carbon Monoxide

All cooking and heating appliances can produce carbon monoxide if not properly ventilated.

Carbon monoxide poisoning can be deadly. The first signs are headaches, tiredness, sickness, and dizziness. It is recommended that you fit a carbon monoxide detector and test it regularly.

To ensure adequate ventilation throughout the cabin, make sure that any ventilators are clear of obstructions.

Using the Heads

There are many different types of marine lavatory (heads). The one shown below is fairly common. The skipper will usually show the crew how the heads work when you come aboard – if not, it's best to ask.

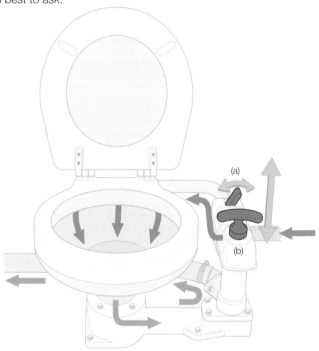

1. To flush, ensure both sea cocks are open – inlet and outlet. Use the toilet.

2. Move the small lever (a) on the pump to the left and pump with the handle (b) about 10 times to suck water in and discharge the contents into the holding tank.

3. Move the lever (a) to the right and pump the bowl dry with handle (b).

4. When out at sea the tank can be bypassed and the toilet used direct to sea.

5. When the tank becomes full, it can be emptied at a specialised pump-out point or out at sea – see local regulations.

Marine toilets rarely get blocked if you follow the instructions, but the pipes are much smaller than at home.These types of items, however, will almost certainly block them. Do not flush them.

Living Afloat

- Stow all gear securely.
- Shut all lockers and hatches.
- Only keep one chart on the chart table with no drinks or wet gear.

- Clean up spills in the galley immediately.
- Put things away in the right place.
- Don't waste water or electricity.
- If on a passage, let off-watch crew get some rest.

Weather Forecasts

Shipping forecast areas

There are many different ways to obtain a forecast. It is always good to follow the weather in the days leading up to your trip to get a balanced view.

Maritime safety information is broadcast on VHF by the Coastguard. For details of forecast times and areas, look in an almanac or the book RYA Weather Forecasts (G5)

The internet – perhaps for many the easiest answer.

Met Office fax.

Smartphone apps.

Recorded forecasts by phone.

Many harbour and marina offices post a forecast.

National and local radio stations.

Beaufort Wind Scale

A forecast wind speed can be affected by local conditions and any tidal conditions.

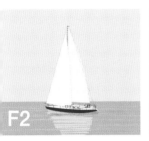

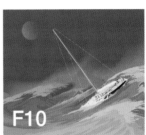

1. Light airs 1–3 knots
Ripples
Sail – drifting conditions

2. Light breeze 4–6 knots
Small wavelets
Sail – full mainsail and large genoa

3. Gentle breeze 7–10 knots
Occasional crests
Sail – full sail

4. Moderate 11–16 knots
Frequent white horses
Sail – reduce headsail size

5. Fresh breeze 17–21 knots
Moderate waves, many white crests
Sail – reef mainsail

6. Strong breeze 22–27 knots
Large waves, white foam crests
Sail – reef main and reduce headsail

7. Near gale 28–33 knots
Sea heaps up, spray, breaking waves,
foam blows in streaks
Sail – deep-reefed main, small jib

8. Gale 34–40 knots
Moderately high waves, breaking crests
Sail – deep-reefed main, storm jib

9. Severe gale 41–47 knots
High waves, spray affects visibility
Sail – trysail and storm jib

10. Storm 48–55 knots
Very high waves, long breaking crests.
Survival conditions

THE ESSENTIALS OF SUSTAINABLE BOATING

An awareness of the environment around you and how to reduce the impact of boating activities part and parcel of being a responsible boater. Looking after our coastal waters will help keep us free of red tape and enable us to continue to enjoy the marine environment, whether cruising o racing, both now and in the future.

FOLLOW THE GREEN BLUE'S TEN ESSENTIAL HABITS TO PREVENT POLLUTION AND MINIMISE DISTURBANCE!

 Refuel using a fuel collar around the fuel nozzle to catch spills and splashes. Avoid overfilling the tank an room for the fuel to expand.

 Have a spill kit to hand in case you need to mop up spills from the deck, fuel berth, or water. Do not use washing up liquid as this disperses the spill into smaller beads that enter the water column.

 Check the engine for leaks to prevent an oily bilge. Install a bilge filter to collect oil, or place a bilge sock bilge to absorb pollutants before pumping the bilge. Dispose of oil collected and the sock in hazardous w facilities found at most harbours and marinas.

 Only discharge the heads when more than 3 miles offshore. Use shorebased toilets when berthed. Use pump out facilities if the boat has a holding tank. Never empty the heads in areas with low tidal flushing.

 Grey water (wastewater) from showers, washbasins, and galley sinks can contain pollutants. Whatever y put down the plughole will end up in the sea, so don't pour away fat, oil, or harmful cleaning products.

 Use phosphate free detergents and cleaners, and avoid bleach, ammonia, and chlorine.

 Keep a tidy, safe boat. Don't let litter go over the side. Even orange peel can take two years to break dow the sea. Try to avoid using single use plastics and use sustainably sourced products where possible.

 Check to see if the area is protected by law or in an environmentally sensitive area before you drop anch

 Watch out for invasive species that harm native species, cause damage to equipment, and can restrict navigation. Wash off your anchor and chain before stowing and leaving an anchorage so you don't sprea species to another location. When removing biofouling from your boat, equipment, and clothing, capture and dispose of in a bin.

 Navigate with care around wildlife. Keep a distance of 100m+ and don't chase or harass. Boaters can be prosecuted (under the Wildlife and Countryside Act 1981, Amended) for disturbing protected wildlife whether intentional or not. Ignorance of the law is not an excuse.

For more information on how to make your boating more environmentally sustainable, download The Gr Guide to Coastal Boating, and The Green Wildlife Guide for Boaters from the 'RYA eBooks' app and visit T Green Blue website for further information and resources.

The Green Blue is the joint environmental programme of the Royal Yachting Association and British Marine created in 2005 to advise and support the UK recreational boating community to minimise any impact on the environment.

www.thegreenblue.or

NOTES

RYA Training Courses

r all ages, abilities and aspirations

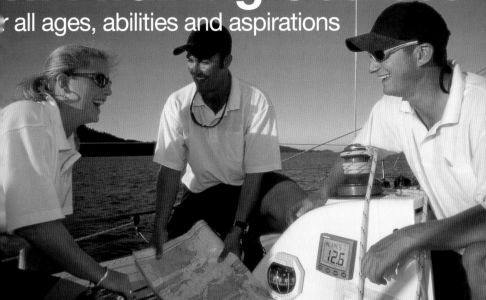

Get the most from your time on the water with our range of practical and shorebased courses.

cruising from the inners' Start Yachting rse to Yachtmaster®

Motor cruising from the introductory Helmsman's course to Yachtmaster®

j Away School of Sailing

Graham Snook/MBM

Shop online at
www.rya.org.uk/shop

- Secure online ordering
- 15% discount for RYA members
- Books, DVDs, navigation aids and lots more
- Free delivery to a UK address for RYA members on orders over £25
- Free delivery to an overseas address for RYA members on orders over £50
- Buying online from the RYA shop enables the RYA in its work on behalf of its members